A FROZEN GUIDE TO MUSIC

Explore Rhythm, Keys, and More

Written by
Tara Flandreau

Illustrated by
the Disney Storybook Art Team

Lerner Publications ◆ Minneapolis

Lerner Publications Company
An imprint of Lerner Publishing Group, Inc.
241 First Avenue North
Minneapolis, MN 55401 USA

For reading levels and more information, look up this title at www.lernerbooks.com.

Main body text set in Italian Old Style MT Std.
Typeface provided by Monotype Typography.

Library of Congress Cataloging-in-Publication Data
Names: Flandreau, Tara.
Title: A Frozen guide to music : explore rhythm, keys, and more / Tara Flandreau.
Description: Minneapolis : Lerner Publications, [2019] | Series: Disney learning let's explore music | Audience: Grade K–3 | Includes index.
Identifiers: LCCN 2019016941 (print) | LCCN 2019017138 (ebook) | ISBN 9781541562226 (eb pdf) | ISBN 9781541554924 (lb : alk. paper) | ISBN 9781541574717 (pb : alk. paper)
Subjects: LCSH: Music theory—Elementary works.
Classification: LCC MT7 (ebook) | LCC MT7 .F68 2019 (print) | DDC 781.2—dc23

LC record available at https://lccn.loc.gov/2019016941

Manufactured in the United States of America
1-45810-42692-5/2/2019

Contents

THIS BOOK will take you on a musical journey

with your friends from *Frozen*. You will learn about **pitch**,
note names on both the **keyboard** and the **staff**, **beats**,
and **more**.

You will need a **keyboard** for some of the activities in this book. There are many free keyboard apps available to download on a tablet or smartphone. Please ask an adult for help in choosing and downloading your favorite app.

Now, let's make some music!

Pitch:
High and Low

Some things make **high** sounds.
A trumpet makes a high sound.
An oboe makes a high sound.
A whistling teakettle makes a high sound.

Some things make **low** sounds.
A tuba makes a low sound.
A reindeer like Sven makes a low sound.
Thunder makes a low sound.

Which things make **high** sounds?

Which things make **low** sounds?

Some things can make both
high and **low** sounds.
A piano can make many high
and low sounds.

Low notes are on the left side of a keyboard.
High notes are on the right side.

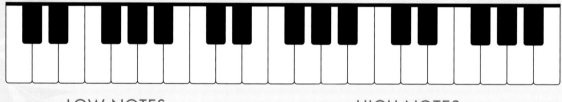

LOW NOTES   HIGH NOTES

Many instruments make both high and low sounds.

Which instruments make both high and low sounds?

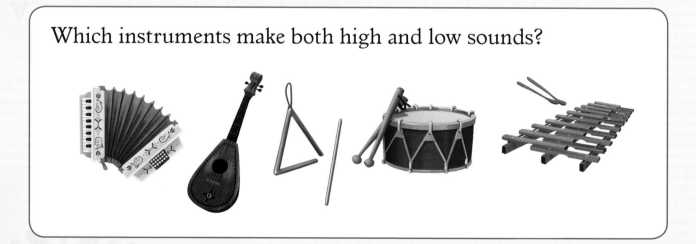

♪ Make Some Music

Try out some high and low sounds on your keyboard.

Choose two notes, one **high** and one **low**. Play the high note with a finger on your right hand. Play the low note with a finger on your left hand.

Follow the chart below to play high, low, long, and short notes.

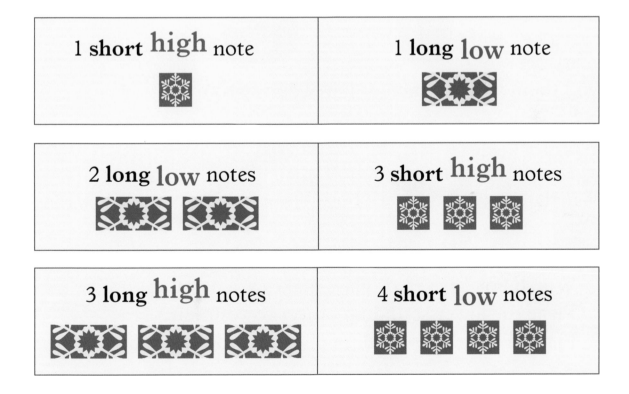

1 short high note	**1 long low note**
2 long low notes	**3 short high notes**
3 long high notes	**4 short low notes**

Make Some Music

Find two pots, buckets, or glasses that are different sizes. Turn them upside down.

Tap them with a pencil or a wooden spoon.

Which pot, bucket, or glass makes a **higher** sound?
Which pot, bucket, or glass makes a **lower** sound?
Place the lower-sounding object to your left.
Place the higher-sounding object to your right.

Follow the chart below to play low and high sounds on the pots, buckets, or glasses.

means play the **low** sound.

means play the **high** sound.

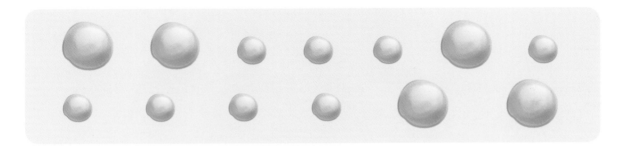

The Keyboard:
Black and White Keys

The keyboard has lots of keys.
It has **black keys**.
It has **white keys**.

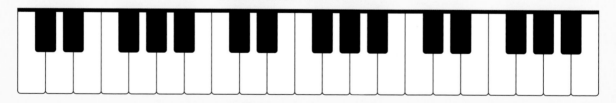

Olaf has a group of 2 carrots and a group of 3 carrots.
The **black keys** on a keyboard are in groups of 2s and 3s.

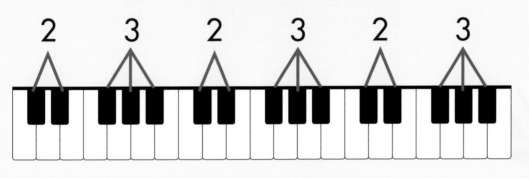

Which keyboards show 2 **black keys**?

 **Make Some Music**

Left hand: Choose a black key from any group of 2 black keys.

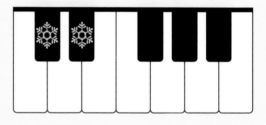

Right hand: Choose a black key from any group of 3 black keys.

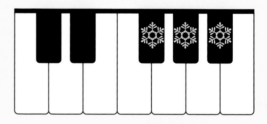

Play the left key alone.
Play the right key alone.
Play the two keys at the same time.

Choose two different keys and play them alone and then together. Can you make a tune with the keys you just chose?

Find a group of two black keys.
Find the white key in between the black keys.

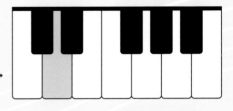

Play the three notes from low to high.
Black, white, black, going up.

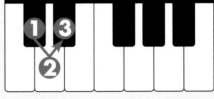

Play the same three notes from high to low.
Black, white, black, going down.

Find a group of three black keys.
There are two white keys in between them.

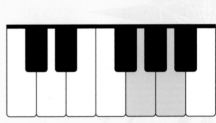

Play the five notes from low to high.
Black, white, black, white, black, going up.

Play the same five notes from high to low.
Black, white, black, white, black, going down.

The Staff

Lines

This is a musical **staff**. It has **5 lines**.
Count the lines up from the bottom: *1, 2, 3, 4, 5.*

Spaces

A musical **staff** also has **spaces**.
Count the **spaces** up from the bottom: *1, 2, 3, 4.*

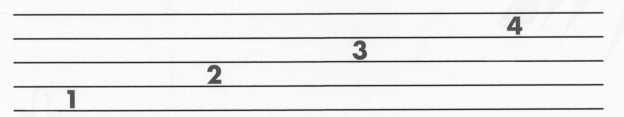

Low and High

When a note is low on the staff, it makes a **low** sound.
When a note is high on the staff, it makes a **high** sound.

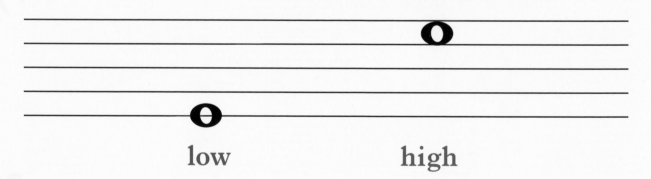

low   high

When you read music, it's important to notice when notes are **lower** and **higher**.

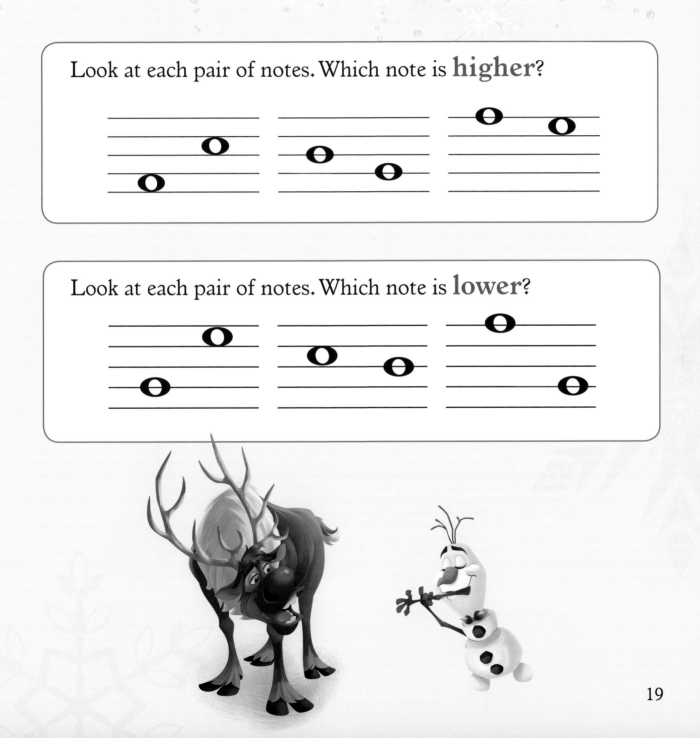

Look at each pair of notes. Which note is **higher**?

Look at each pair of notes. Which note is **lower**?

Make Some Music

Find three glasses that are the same size and shape.

Fill the first glass nearly to the top with water. This is your blue glass.

Fill the second glass about halfway with water. This is your red glass.

Fill the third glass with a small amount of water. This is your green glass.

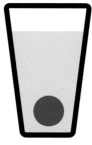  

Tap each glass lightly with a spoon. The glasses make three different notes.

The blue glass makes the lowest note.

The red glass makes the middle note.

The green glass makes the highest note.

Here are some notes that go up on the staff.
Notes that go up are called **ascending** notes.

Play ascending notes on the glasses.

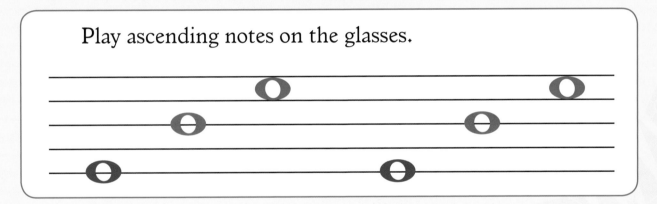

Here are some notes that go down on the staff.
Notes that go down are called **descending** notes.

Play descending notes on the glasses.

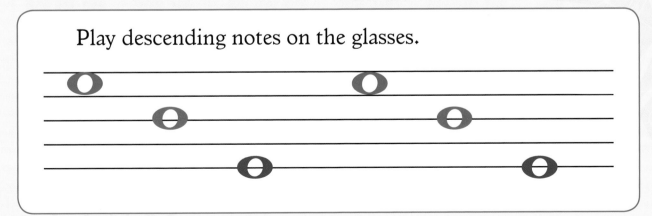

Note Names on the Keyboard

There are seven letters, or **note names**, for musical notes—**A**, **B**, **C**, **D**, **E**, **F**, and **G**. They go up the white keys of the keyboard. When we run out of **note names**, we use the same ones over and over again.

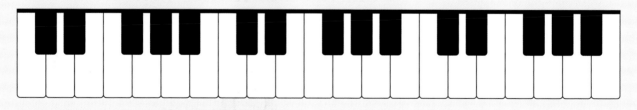

Look at the **note names** on the keyboard.
After **G** comes **A** again.
The **note names** keep repeating, over and over.

What are the missing **note names**?

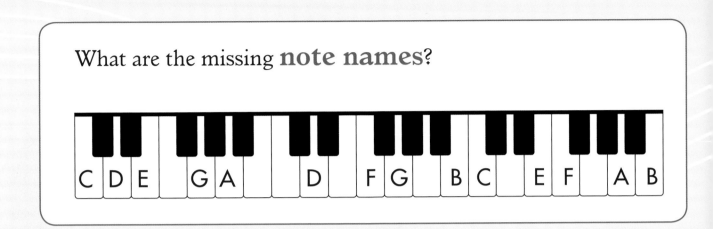

 **Make Some Music**

Find a group of two black keys.
There is a white key in between them.
This is the note **D**.
Play all the **D**s on your keyboard.

The white key just to the left of **D** is **C**.
C is an important note.
Play all the **C**s on your keyboard.

Which note names should go on the white keys?

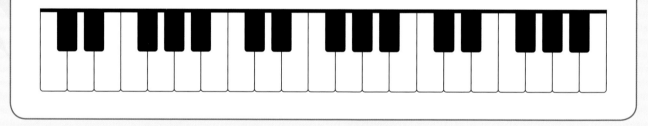

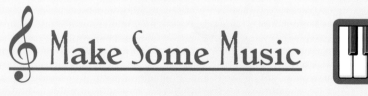 **Make Some Music**

Play the white keys from low to high.
Say the letter name of each note out loud as you play it.

Some keys are marked with snowflakes.
On a separate sheet of paper, write their note names.
What words did you spell?

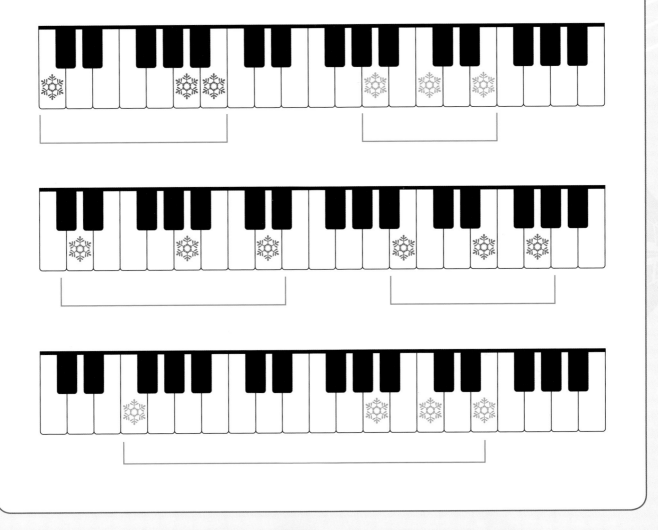

Note Names on the Staff

This is a **treble clef**. It helps us know where notes are on the staff. The spiral part always curls around the second line. The note on that line is **G**.

These are the **note names** on the staff in treble clef.

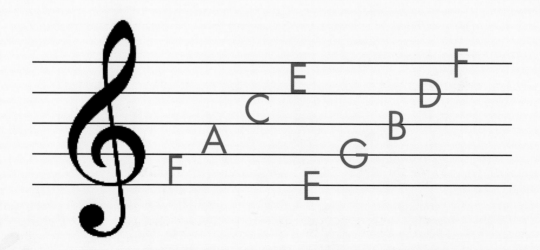

The **note names** in the **spaces** are easy to remember.
The **note names** in the **spaces** spell F A C E.

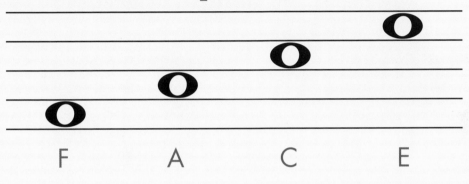

F   A   C   E

The **note names** on the **lines** don't spell anything. But we can
use words to help remember the **note names** on the **lines**.

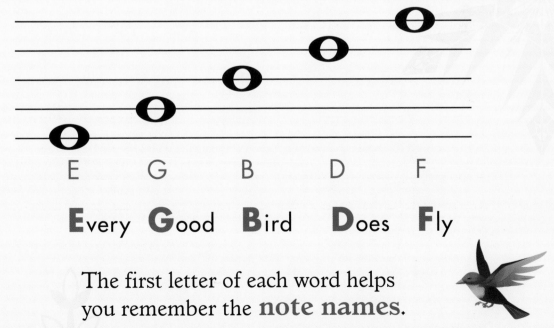

E   G   B   D   F

Every **G**ood **B**ird **D**oes **F**ly

The first letter of each word helps
you remember the **note names**.

Beats

Some notes last for a long time.
Some notes last for a short time.

We can tap **beats** to measure the **length** of notes.

Beats sound just like seconds ticking on a clock—*tick, tick, tick.* They also sound like the beats of your heart—*thump, thump, thump.*

Say this rhyme and clap your hands to the **beat**. Clap when you see a ❆ for the beat.

❆   ❆ ❆   ❆

Rock-a-bye, baby, on the treetop.

❆   ❆ ❆   ❆

When the wind blows, the cradle will rock.

❆   ❆ ❆   ❆

When the bough breaks, the cradle will fall.

❆   ❆ ❆   ❆

And down will come baby, cradle and all.

Say this rhyme and clap your hands to the **beat**.
Clap when you see a ❄ for the beat.

❄ ❄ ❄ ❄

This old man, he played one.

❄ ❄ ❄ ❄

He played knick-knack on my thumb.

❄ ❄ ❄ ❄

With a knick-knack, paddywhack, give a dog a bone,

❄ ❄ ❄ ❄

This old man came rolling home.

Sometimes there are silent beats that happen when we are not singing. Say this rhyme and clap your hands to the **beat**.
Clap when you see a ❄ for the beat.

❄ ❄ ❄ ❄

Hickory, dickory, dock.

❄ ❄ ❄ ❄

The mouse ran up the clock.

❄ ❄ ❄ ❄

The clock struck one, the mouse ran down,

❄ ❄ ❄ ❄

Hickory, dickory, dock.

Simple Note Values

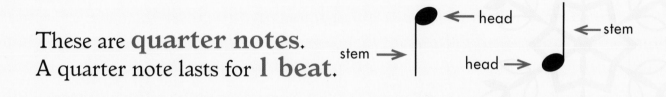

Each type of note lasts for a different number of **beats**.

These are **quarter notes**.
A quarter note lasts for **1 beat**.

head
stem
stem
head

These are **half notes**.
A half note lasts for **2 beats**.
It is twice as long as a quarter note.

head
stem
stem
head

This is a **whole note**.
It lasts for **4 beats**.
It is twice as long as a half note.
It is 4 times as long as a quarter note.

head

Music Math

Add the notes together.
How many **beats** are there in all?

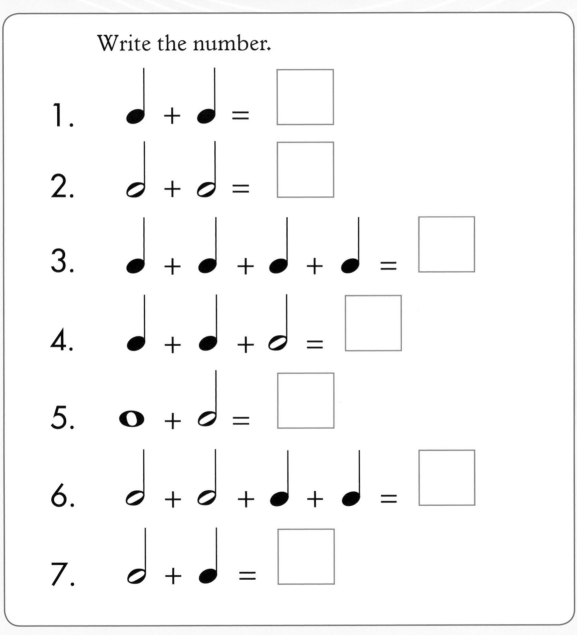

Write the number.

1. ♩ + ♩ = ☐

2. ♩ + ♩ = ☐

3. ♩ + ♩ + ♩ + ♩ = ☐

4. ♩ + ♩ + ♩ = ☐

5. 𝅝 + ♩ = ☐

6. ♩ + ♩ + ♩ + ♩ = ☐

7. ♩ + ♩ = ☐

You've learned a lot about music! Use what you've learned to keep practicing, playing, and creating!

Answers: 1. 2 beats; 2. 4 beats; 3. 4 beats; 4. 4 beats; 5. 6 beats; 6. 6 beats; 7. 3 beats

Glossary

ascending: going upward. Ascending notes go up the staff.

beat: how long to hold a note

descending: going downward. Descending notes go down the staff.

pitch: how high or low a note is

staff: the lines you use to write music

treble clef: a symbol that goes on the staff. It helps you know where notes are.

Index